Volume 62 of the Yale Series of Younger Poets, edited by Dudley Fitts and published with aid from the Mary Cady Tew Memorial Fund.

The Lost Pilot

by James Tate

Foreword by Dudley Fitts

New Haven and London

Yale University Press

1967

Acknowledgment is made to the following publications for poems which originally appeared in them:

Ante: Prelude to a Glass City *Atlantic Monthly:* The Last Letter from Old Kampoukos; The Lost Pilot; Reapers of the Water *Boston Review:* Crepuscule with Fatima; Flight *Dust:* Manna *Heartland: Poets of the Midwest* (Northern Illinois University Press): Aunt Edna; The End of the Line; Late Harvest; Intimidations of an Autobiography; In a Town for Which I Know No Name; The Loveliest Woman in Altoona, Iowa; The Sunday Driver in Search of Himself; Uncle *Kayak:* How the Friends Met; The Face of the Waters; Late Harvest; Self-Portrait with Demons; Still Movement in Reflection; Today I Am Falling *Manhattan Review:* Miss Cho Composes in the Cafeteria *North American Review:* The Butcher with Nothing but Bones; Closing the Chamber Doors; Epithalamion for Tyler; Saint Vitus's Dance; The Shop Keeper *The Poetry Bag:* Uncle *Shenandoah:* For Mother on Father's Day

Library of Congress catalog card number: 67–13449

To Kathryn

Foreword

A natural grace is as rare in poetry as it is anywhere else. Certainly it is the last quality, except perhaps for metrical literacy, that an editor can expect to find as he picks his way through the aspiring manuscripts, and the impact of it when it comes may jolt his sense of proportion. My initial impression of Mr James Tate's poems will serve as an instance. 'A robust amused declarative style': such was my first notation, which added 'weird and substantial' as a reaction to 'Coming Down Cleveland Avenue' and 'Rescue'; and it underlies the more complicated responses that a growing familiarity with this young poet's range has brought. I mean a gaiety, a fresh, unselfconscious way of perceiving and recording, though that the work as a whole has darker and more disturbing reaches than these amiable traits suggest will be denied by no one who ponders the title poem and others of its calibre. The substance is inevitably there, however exuberant the manner. It is nevertheless the vigorous freshness of Mr Tate's invention that continues to pique the imagination.

I have mentioned 'Rescue', a poem that may be taken as characteristic. It is a love poem, and in its sixteen lines it quietly accepts and affirms the enormous perils of physical engagement:

> *For the first time the only*
> *thing you are likely to break*
>
> *is everything because*
> *it is a dangerous*
>
> *venture. Danger invites*
> *rescue —*

Economical and lean enough. The poet is both involved and standing apart from the action of the moment. But there is a tenderness, too, and the wit of a happy initiation; and therein lies the grace of which I have spoken. There is no ornamentation, although the modulations of cadence achieved by the lineation, the spacing of caesurae, and the interbalance of distichs attest to the amount of conscious art that has gone into the construction. The figurative element is as unadorned:

> *There is plenty of room,*
> *clean windows, we start our best*
>
> *engines, a-rumm ... everything is*
> *relevant –*

Everything is indeed relevant. The brave tone is as solidly based as it was honestly earned, yet there is no sense of strain, no trace whatever of the fashionable cleverness in sex that bores us all. (As an exercise it would be interesting to investigate the effect of the space between the second and third of the lines just quoted, and to think through the wry comedy of 'engines, a-rumm'; but a brief introductory note must forgo these pleasures.) In any event, the perils of loving that 'invite rescue' parallel the perils of sensibility that invite poetry: the poem is like the lover's confidence that all these dangers and difficulties, exorcised by one form of art or another, will disappear. And comedy, when it is relevant, is a potent form of art.

Not that Mr Tate's poems are comic, except in the older technical sense of the word: that is to say, that they confirm joy, not disgust. It is true that the picture of

> *trepid riding*
> *Tate (gone loco in the*
> *cabeza)*

is an engaging one, and we find equally attractive images in the odd and long – probably too long – 'The Last Letter from Old Kampoukos', in 'The Butcher with Nothing but Bones', and in the giddy *bourrée surréaliste* with which 'Coming Down Cleveland Avenue' concludes:

> *But pretty*
> *soon your darling jumps*
> *out of an elevator*
> *and kisses you and you*
> *sing and tell her to*
> *walk the white plains*
> *proudly. At one point*
> *you even lay down*
> *your coat, and she, in*
> *turn, puts hers down for*
> *you. And you put your*
> *shirt down, and she, her*
> *blouse, and your pants,*
> *and her skirt, shoes —*
> *removes her lavender*
> *underwear and you slip*
> *into her proud, white skin.*

At the beginning I was so taken by this last poem that I would have staked the entire book on it, and I was at any rate successful in persuading the author – who was reluctant, finding the piece 'untypical' – to move it up to first place from somewhere in the middle of his manuscript. The infatuations of editorship? It may be so; yet if the poem is untypical of Mr Tate, in the sense that it lacks the stringent resonances of 'The Lost Pilot', it serves me nevertheless as a paradigm of what I find new and chiefly valuable in the book as a whole. 'Clean windows,' says Mr Tate; 'With wash'd eyes,' says Lear's Cordelia. This poet sees with washed eyes, or so it seems to me; he sees cleanly, with a gusty freshness that makes possible the most illuminating strokes of invention. This kind of clarity has its dangers, as 'Rescue' implies; I suppose that one could postulate a trepid riding clarity; but

> *A man would wrestle*
> *with his soul, and all*

the other sinners cheered,
and soon we heard
the voices of another tongue –

garbled, and far too
inflated for us
to understand who

taught them how to sing such songs.

The dangers have dispersed themselves. What emerges finally is a body of young poetry, utterly new – James Tate sounds to me like no one I have ever read –, utterly confident, with an effortless elegance of control, both in diction and in composition, that would be rare in a poet of any age and that is particularly impressive in a first book. I do not know who taught him how to sing such songs. It is enough for me that he is singing them, and that it is my privilege to pass the first of them on.

Dudley Fitts

Contents

II

III

*Where did it all go wrong? There ought to be a law
against Henry.
— Mr. Bones: there is.*

John Berryman

Coming Down Cleveland Avenue

The fumes from all kinds
of machines have dirtied
the snow. You propose
to polish it, the miles
between home and wherever
you and your lily
of a woman might go. You
go, pail, brush, and
suds, scrubbing down
Cleveland Avenue
toward the Hartford Life
Insurance Company. No
one appreciates your
effort and one important
character calls you
a baboon. But pretty
soon your darling jumps
out of an elevator
and kisses you and you
sing and tell her to
walk the white plains
proudly. At one point
you even lay down
your coat, and she, in
turn, puts hers down for
you. And you put your
shirt down, and she, her
blouse, and your pants,
and her skirt, shoes —
removes her lavender
underwear and you slip
into her proud, white skin.

3

The Shop Keeper

There is a word for it,
A simple word,
And the word goes around.
                    Donald Justice

It is too early to close up
the shop, but you are tired and it
shows – you just broke a two dollar
thing. God only knows how these things
keep breaking. Now you think you know.

You close the door and leave to find
your home. Afraid to think of what
business is coming to, you
think of sleep, dishwater, gaslamps,
cypress, eggshells, hell; what you are

coming to – bells, rags, big Sunday.
Anxious to find your house, perhaps
laden with mail, monuments, sin,
eyelashes. You feel like a woman,
like a basement tobacco shop,

a busted fountain, a sloppy
staircase. Dark, damp lists of words, you
say them. One will say it all
soon. Then you will not have to sweep
up in the morning. The two dollars

will be well invested – barrel
organ, german ladies, tug-of-war,
arithmetic, geraniums. . . .

4

Reapers of the Water

The nets newly tarred
and the family arranged
on deck – Mass has started.

The archbishop in
his golden
cope and tall miter, a resplendent

figure against an unwonted background, the darting
silver of water,
green and lavender

of the hyacinths, the slow
movement of occasional
boats. Incense floats

up and about the dripping gray
moss and the sound of the altar bell
rings out. Automatically all who have stayed

on their boats drop to their knees with the others
on shore. The prelate, next taking up his sermon,
recalls that the disciples of Christ were drawn

from the fishermen
of Galilee. Through
the night, at the lake, they cast in vain.

Then He told
them to try once more, and lo!
the nets came heavily loaded. . . . Now

there will be days when
you, too, will
cast your nets without success – be not

discouraged; His all-seeing
eye will be
on you. And in the storm, when

your boat tosses like a thin
leaf, hold firm. . . .
Who knows whose man will be next? Grand'mère

whose face describes how three of hers –
her husband and those two boys – had not returned,
now looks toward

her last son –
it is a matter of time.
The prelate dips his gold aspergillum

into the container of holy water
and lifts it high. As the white
and green boats

pass, the drops fall on the scrubbed
decks, on the nets, on the shoulders
of the nearest ones, and they move up

the long waterway.
The crowds watching and waving:
the *Sea Dream,* the *Normandie,*

the *Barbara Coast,* the *Little Hot
Dog,* the *God
Bless America,* the *Madame of Q.*–

racing past the last tendrils
of the warm pudding
that is Louisiana.

6

Epithalamion for Tyler

I thought I knew something
about loneliness but
you go to the stockyards

buy a pig's ear and sew
it on your couch. That, you
said, is my best friend – we

have spirited talks. Even
then I thought: a man of
such exquisite emptiness

(and you cultivated it so)
is ground for fine flowers.

For Mother on Father's Day

You never got to recline
in the maternal tradition,
I never let you. Fate,

you call it, had other eyes,
for neither of us ever had
a counterpart in the way

familial traditions go.
I was your brother,
and you were my unhappy

neighbor. I pitied you
the way a mother pities
her son's failure. I could

never find the proper
approach. I would have
lent you sugar, mother.

8

In a Town for Which I Know No Name

I think of your blind odor
too long till I collide with
barbers, and am suspected.

The clerk malingers when I
nod. I am still afraid of
the natural. Even the

decrepit animals,
coveting their papers and
curbs, awake and go breathing

through the warm darkness of
hotel halls. I think that they
are you coming back from the

colossal obscurity
of your exhausted passions,
and dash to the door again.

The Butcher with Nothing but Bones

You touch the window,
certainly it is
there. You are having
a very good time
touching the window,
imagining what
is hiding behind.

There, the regally
garmented coquette
cautiously drops by,
feeling the window
pane too, blind to your
vigil. She is the
good friend just arrived
in the nick of time.

What would you give for
the right size rock? When
wearing the window
away with your nose,
the window grows. Your
lips are finally
rocks, and the window
keeps growing. She is
just fine. She is just
being crushed. She is
just your kind of girl.

Crepuscule with Fatima

The smoke no more
festoons in hexagons:
with dawn, our kings

become invisible,
and we serfs, anxious
to tend our flowers,

are left wondering
where we found
such royalty.

Fatima, here, says
to liquidate time
and space should not

be held against us –
what if a flower
should bleed? Blue air

comprehends
the phenomenal. So,
we sacrifice a sense

or two that only
served to sanctify
a great misunderstanding.

We need no common
senses when we walk
out of our red eyes

to greet the sun.
These featherbrains
with purple garlands

pirate the crown jewels
from the newborn sky.

Stopping by the Bridge on a Snowy Evening

Waiting for you to explain,
we sit and wait, but what
do you say, you who wear

yourself out suffering
for us? You cry and embrace
a parapet. An angry cripple

informs you, we can carry
our own burdens. Not that you
have an evil heart —

low ceilings and cramped rooms
have crushed your mind
and spirit. You look like

a spider going to Golgotha.
Flame-colored creatures,
we watch your eerie machinations;

weakling, we judge you
and your furious red bath.
The wet snow is falling

face-first without wind
or discrimination.
Like a sticky leaf, greenish

and sickly, you never open.
You desire to walk not
with us, but on black waters

for us. And, when the glassy
gleam of the moon drew you
with her white eyelashes

continually winking, you
leaped, falling in dizzy
spirals like smoke of

an upside-down cigar.
The inside of a river
you found to be

a very unventilated room.

The Hermit

The furtive, begifted ladies
in bright-colored itchy shawls
hammer the boulevards
in a diminishing circle.

From the mountainside,
I watch their fallen faces
rise, and scarcely believe
the luck I have had.

Still Movement in Reflection

These hands consider
stillness a giving
in. I dreamed I had

to watch a handshake
chipped from the floor of
the Arctic Ocean

eternally this
afternoon and the
possibility

of something still worse
never occurred. I
was stupefied but

not alarmed. I did
not dream that when
I died my ankles

became the pillars
of shopping centers.
That was a relief. I

am only trying
to make you stop. Have
you ever? Here come

the fears, vortical
fugitive vagrant
panoramas. They

are all that I own.
Take them. Always your
happiness in mind.

Success Comes to Cow Creek

I sit on the tracks,
a hundred feet from
earth, fifty from the
water. Gerald is
inching toward me
as grim, slow, and
determined as a
season, because he
has no trade and wants
none. It's been nine months
since I last listened
to his fate, but I
know what he will say:
he's the fire hydrant
of the underdog.

When he reaches my
point above the creek,
he sits down without
salutation, and
spits profoundly out
past the edge, and peeks
for meaning in the
ripple it brings. He
scowls. He speaks: when you
walk down any street
you see nothing but
coagulations
of shit and vomit,
and I'm sick of it.
I suggest suicide;
he prefers murder,

and spits again for
the sake of all the
great devout losers.

A conductor's horn
concerto breaks the
air, and we, two doomed
pennies on the track,
shove off and somersault
like anesthetized
fleas, ruffling the
ideal locomotive
poised on the water
with our light, dry bodies.
Gerald shouts
terrifically as
he sails downstream like
a young man with a
destination. I
swim toward shore as
fast as my boots will
allow; as always,
neglecting to drown.

The Face of the Waters

Perhaps I have only remained;
stood still, beautiful, and
(as a sagacious friend once

said) with a deep yearning
for the ascetic existence.
I was reading Meister Eckhart

at the time because I wanted
my friends to think I was
beautiful and had a deep

yearning for the ascetic etcetera.
Modes of advertising changed.
Selling yourself, I said,

condescending from the bottom
of a dream. What is this
springing from the ground?

Rain? Kings and queens
donkeying through the fractured
gallery of my seasons.

At least this is not the rain
I requested. Another bad
shipment due to nevermind.

The streets are alive with
free swimming animals: fiddler
crabs, coelenterates, river

otters, venus flower baskets –
I know you are out there
but you cannot come in.

Why I Will Not Get Out of Bed

My muscles unravel
like spools of ribbon:
there is not a shadow

of pain. I will pose
like this for the rest
of the afternoon,

for the remainder
of all noons. The rain
is making a valley

of my dim features.
I am in Albania,
I am on the Rhine.

It is autumn,
I smell the rain,
I see children running

through columbine.
I am honey,
I am several winds.

My nerves dissolve,
my limbs wither –
I don't love you.

I don't love you.

The Descent

I imagine that these thousand
sleek, invisible zebras are
leading me somewhere;

it is the moment before
birth, I expect, and follow.
The air that pursues us

is as warm and moist
as the breath of a young
rhinoceros. The sky rumbles

with televisions. Harry
Langdon in *The Life
of Abu Bakr*. None of the little

anthracite rabbits with carrot
pink eyes are real.
I know that now and feel

burdened with all the eternal
verities. The ground beneath me
is as soft as the tongue

of an old giraffe. Where
are we now, darlings? This
suitcase has lost its charm.

Graveside

Rodina Feldervatova,
the community's black angel –
well, we come to you,

having failed to sink
our own webbed fingers
in the chilled earth where

you hang out. I think
you are doomed to become
symbols for us that we

will never call by name.
But what rifles through
our heads is silence, one

either beyond or below
whatever it is that we do
know. We know by heart,

don't we? We've never
learned. And we bring what
we have known to you, now,

tonight. Open your home
to us, Rodina. Kiss
our brains. Tell us that

we are not drunk, and
that we may spend
our summers with you.

Pastoral Scene

The wind makes a salad
of the countryside and
he who is so hungry
sits down but refuses
to eat greens. Nearby, the
river is a truck in
a hurry. He won't go
with it, however. The game
he has come to kill come
to watch him hunt himself
now. They have never felt
so safe before, so out
of place. An old predator
at last chewing on himself
is a ridiculous sight,
and the peeping white deer
are happier than they
have ever been before.

The Cages

The insular firebird
(meaning the sun) gives up
the day, and is tucked into

a corner. Order, like
a giant janitor, shuttles
about naming and replacing

the various humanities.
I look at you, you look
at me – we wave again

(the same), our hands like
swollen flags falling, words
marooned in the brain.

Tyler Remembers

I found marriage
acceptable; her dull dry
hair shifting like bramble kept

the incomprehensible
silences of the morning
hours bearable. The feelings

of nothing everywhere
were lessened; her little
brittle voice was almost there

always, and never was.
Her phantom words, that music
which I nearly heard, still hang

here like the thrilling
anticipation of some
easy and elemental death.

Of my wife my memory
labors, deep beckoning sounds.
My voice? I have forgotten.

The Lost Pilot

for my father, 1922–1944

Your face did not rot
like the others – the co-pilot,
for example, I saw him

yesterday. His face is corn-
mush: his wife and daughter,
the poor ignorant people, stare

as if he will compose soon.
He was more wronged than Job.
But your face did not rot

like the others – it grew dark,
and hard like ebony;
the features progressed in their

distinction. If I could cajole
you to come back for an evening,
down from your compulsive

orbiting, I would touch you,
read your face as Dallas,
your hoodlum gunner, now,

with the blistered eyes, reads
his braille editions. I would
touch your face as a disinterested

scholar touches an original page.
However frightening, I would
discover you, and I would not

26

turn you in; I would not make
you face your wife, or Dallas,
or the co-pilot, Jim. You

could return to your crazy
orbiting, and I would not try
to fully understand what

it means to you. All I know
is this: when I see you,
as I have seen you at least

once every year of my life,
spin across the wilds of the sky
like a tiny, African god,

I feel dead. I feel as if I were
the residue of a stranger's life,
that I should pursue you.

My head cocked toward the sky,
I cannot get off the ground,
and, you, passing over again,

fast, perfect, and unwilling
to tell me that you are doing
well, or that it was mistake

that placed you in that world,
and me in this; or that misfortune
placed these worlds in us.

Intimidations of an Autobiography

I am walking a trail
on a friend's farm
about three miles from

town. I arrange the day
for you. I stop and say,
you would not believe how happy

I was as a child,
to some logs. Blustery wind
puts tumbleweed

in my face as I am
pretending to be on my way
home to see you and

the family again,
to touch the orange
fingers of the moon.

That's how I think of it.
The years flipped back last night
and I drank hot rum till

dawn.
It was a wild success and I wasn't sad when
I woke past noon

and saw the starlings in the sky.
My brain's an old rag anyway,
but I've got a woman and you'd say

she's too good for me. You'd call
her a real doll and me a goof-ball.
I've got my head between my paws

because it's having a damn
birthday party. How old do you think I am?
I bet you think I'm

seventeen.
It doesn't matter. Just between
us, you know what I'm doing

now? I'm calling the cows home.
They're coming, too.
I lower

myself to the ground lazily,
a shower of avuncular kisses
issuing from my hands and lips –

I just wanted to tell you
I remember you even now;
Goodbye, goodbye. Here come the cows.

Self-Portrait with Demons

Through the emerald-
ringed neck of a pheasant
I watch your inauspicious

concern. The gravel road
smells like bacon
at night. Your barn is built

on stilts. There is a lantern;
that is your eye. I am
sorry my car is wavering.

It hauls me. I am not
in control anymore.
That is not a lake.

That is not hay. You
have to watch me
do this to myself now.

Where is my hair
going? Swaddled in wood,
do you accept apologies?

The End of the Line

We plan in partial sleep
a day of intense activity –
to arrive at a final bargain

with the deaf grocer,
to somehow halt a train;
we plan our love's rejuvenation

one last time. And then
she dreams another life
altogether. I've gone away.

The petals of a red bud
caught in a wind between
Hannibal and Carthage,

the day has disappeared.
Like a little soap bubble
the moon glides around

our bed. We are two negroes
lugubriously sprawled
on a parched boardwalk.

The Move

. . . you are alone with the Alone,
and it is His move.

Robert Penn Warren

The old buccaneers are leaving
now. They have had
their fill. A blue halo

has circled the imitation
gold, and the real, and they
are bewildered. All

is shimmering. The sea
is shimmering like a marvelous belly
viewed from the outside

during a blizzard in the mountains.
For each other
they are shimmering.

They do not know what splendor
is balanced
atop the foresail now, what

it is that is moving, moving
toward them, down.
They rub their bodies.

The skin is a fine lace
of salt and disease,
and something is moving

just under the skin
and they know
that it is not blood.

Flight

for K.

Like a glum cricket
the refrigerator is singing
and just as I am convinced

that it is the only noise
in the building, a pot falls
in 2B. The neighbors on

both sides of me suddenly
realize that they have not
made love to their wives

since 1947. The racket
multiplies. The man downhall
is teaching his dog to fly.

The fish are disgusted
and beat their heads blue
against a cold aquarium. I too

lose control and consider
the dust huddled in the corner
a threat to my endurance.

Were you here, we would not
tolerate mongrels in the air,
nor the conspiracies of dust.

We would drive all night,
your head tilted on my shoulder.
At dawn, I would nudge you

with my anxious fingers and say,
Already we are in Idaho.

Grace

The one thing that sustained
the faces on the four
corners of the intersection

did not unite them,
did not invite others to join.
Their inner eyes as the light

changed did not change,
but focused madly precise
on the one thing until

it scared them. Then
they all went to the movies.
I was just beginning

to understand when one
who represented the desperate
shrunken state came toward

me, bisecting the whole mass
of concrete into triangles,
and handed me a package.

I carried it with me for
the rest of my life, never
opening it, telling no one.

Closing the Chamber Doors

His eyes are the artifacts
of a private glacial age.
The doctors have given him

forty years to live, have
given him fifty, but this
morning there were lagoons

of sawfish coiled in
the clock's alarm. Today he
cannot hoist the dishrags

above the secret orifices
of Chicago, for the Dalai Lama
of Menninger's has come

to lead him to his chamber.
As he reports the caterwaul
of bees he has recently

swallowed, the expert, like
an old Navaho squaw, weaves
his sutures, stopping

the lip's incessant flutter.

Saint Vitus's Dance

He puts the pieces
of a thin shell that
he broke in a ditch

and walks on picking
himself a bouquet
that soon explodes in

his hand. Heat moves
beneath him. Above,
ducks convulse and their

blood dries as they fall
on him like a dose
of acid. Eyelashes

of white whales sprinkle
from an abandoned
well that he stares down;

Confederate suits
shift in the cave where,
again, he tries to

stand still; but the ends
of his fingers keep
glowing and burning.

The Last Days of April

Through the ceiling comes
the rain to cool my lover
and me. The lime carpeting

darkens, and when we cross
to retrieve our glasses
of gin from the mantle, our

feet sink as into drifts
of leaves. We have a deep
thirst, for it is the end

of April, and we know that
a great heat is coming soon
to deaden these passions.

II

Uncle

Homer was a ventriloquist;
so drunk, one day he projected his voice
so far it just

kept going and going (still is).
Joe Ray insisted
Homer was afraid of work, but he's

had 130 jobs or more
just recently, he didn't think in terms
of careers.

The family never
cared for Homer
even after

he ginned himself into a wall
and died balling
with a deaf-mute in an empty Kansas City hall.

Joe Ray insisted
Homer would have made a fine dentist
had he kept his mouth shut; that is,

had he lived. Still is
heard about the house
jiggling glasses,

his devoted astral voice coming back.

How the Friends Met

So what do you do? What
can you do? Leave the room
altogether? Crazy.
Your eyes are the wallpaper;
makes it tough, doesn't it?
Peel them away. You call
that pain? It's not. It's insane.

You make it. Keep going.
Confront a lightpole. Smoke
a mythopoeic
cigarette forever.
Mark a spot with your
mysterious shoe; scratch
Hate in the sidewalk.

A man will come along
and there will be reason
enough to knife him. Sure
enough, there comes along
a worse-than-Bogart. . . .
There you are, smoking
the lightpole. The spot

you marked appears between
your eyes, and then becomes
a sidewalk, and the man
walks right up the sidewalk
into your room, looks at
the wallpaper, and laughs.
So what do you do? What

can you do? Kick him out?
Hell, no. You charge him rent.

Nepenthe

Koala, marsupial
arboreal (a female),
two-feet long & sharp claws,
hairy large ears – feeds upon
your eucalyptus leaf heart.

She is your cuddly girl, soft,
and you tell the zoo keepers,
leave my koala alone.
You tell them, she's not for sale,
even though you know she'd bring
right nice laughable profit.

Prelude to a Glass City

Let him scratch the recesses
with fingers as long & black
as the hour, but I prefer
the nonsense left untampered –
my cerebral volcanoes
I have grown fond of; I have
taken a liking to Lear.
He crawls to my boot like a
lame snake: one of us is loony.
Doctor Snake, think I am silly?
Think I show signs, like a
history professor without
time? Didn't think I cared, eh?
Well, listen, I have an idea:
I keep it in a jar: I keep
it in a glass – the laughter
in the glass keeps me alive,
is the icing on my eyes,
the essence of the world, but –
don't quote me. This is all:
A rose is not a cannonball.

The Malingerer

Aunt Dwindle, don't you
care for me? Or a token from
The Underground: all

the rummies got babies;
the noble livers folded up
and stashed in a new cellar.

I would be fascinated;
I like poor taste. Nothing
like a turban; for example,

I wear one to traffic court.
You ought to see me yawn.
I've got a fortune, time.

Who's there? I thought
I heard the lawn shift. If
I had a connection, I would

weasel out of this and that.
You ought to see me smoke;
pollute, pollute – that's me.

I thought I heard the sky squeak.
Oh, it's Nothing, it's Uncle
Nothing coming down from his tree.

Tragedy Comes to the Bad Lands

Amnesic goatherds tromboning
on the summit, the lazy
necklaces of their own breath
evanesce into the worst
blizzard since Theodore
Roosevelt and the Marquis
de Mores blessed Medora, North
Dakota with their rugged
presence. Look! I implore, who's
sashaying across the Bad
Lands now – it's trepid riding
Tate (gone loco in the
cabeza) out of his little
civilized element – Oh!
It's bound to end in tears.

Aunt Edna

Aunt Edna of the hills
comes down to give
her sisters chills;

she wears the same
rags she wore
seven years ago,

she smells
the same, she tells
the same hell-

is-here stories.
She hates flowers,
she hates the glory

of the church she
abandoned for the
glory

of her Ozark cave.
She gave
her sons to the wolves.

The Sunday Driver in Search of Himself

Rolling at eighty, now ninety,
I know why I came here: I was
beginning to feel like a crowd,

you know the ones pinching
each other's fanny, tubercular
wheezing when you turn around.

Whole burping galaxies
of these silly people collecting
inside of me, squeaking,

reeling, until one night, last
night, frozen downtown, I was
trying to recall just where

it was I was going
to meet you, just when, just
who on earth you are. I read

phonebooks, took cabs, waited
in lobbies, ball parks, and
The Tulsa Opera House. Sequinned

ladies, I said, have you seen
the likes of me? Over there,
they said. See, over there. . . .

And, now, here I am, going
lickety-split, hellbound over
mountains, gullies, and water;

and loving, really loving
every mile of it, the knowing
that only you are around.

Violins

She knew how to make a moment famous.
Heifetz plucked a marvelous Sibelius.
Meanwhile, a thunderstorm made sounds
metastatic, like who said God
couldn't beat a mean bass drum?
She even brought me flowers and the rain
slapped and shattered through the screen
making music, more music, far too much –
you get the picture? Violins.
We wrote a dozen poems
before the rainbow came.

Rescue

For the first time the only
thing you are likely to break

is everything because
it is a dangerous

venture. Danger invites
rescue – I call it loving.

We've got a good thing
going – I call it rescue.

Nicest thing ever to come
between steel cobwebs, we hope

so. A few others should get
around to it, I can't understand

it. There is plenty of room,
clean windows, we start our best

engines, a-rumm . . . everything is
relevant. I call it loving.

III

The Loveliest Woman in Altoona, Iowa

Tonight the loveliest woman
in Altoona is giving herself
to a dry-cleaning apprentice

beneath swings in City Park.
His mustard breath, his life,
is crystallizing as he

manipulates her loins,
imagining competence. And then
it happens: her coveted eggs

rush through the earth
like small, ecstatic animals,
and the Midwest contracts

in horror. There is hardly
a place to stand. The entire
village has gathered

to confirm the mayor's prediction:
Gabriella and Barnaby have
come to an evil end. Smoke,

water, and sirens malign
the sky. Surely it will be
broadcast soon that all

is under control, and the elders
will sigh, thinking they
too are under control,

though their lives were exposed
to a crime of passion.
Come see the people writhe.

One Dream of Indians

When I thought of Indians
before, I thought of slender
muscular men with feather

heads wailing hallelujah,
of blood spears on white flesh, their
two-toned ponies insane.

To slit the jugular of
a whole sun-skinned nation is
what I thought I ought to do.

And the leathery women
they left hung with huge papooses –
they were no better; they hugged

the men when they returned with
empty quivers and crooned the
brave who fell. There was one dream

of Indians I didn't
dream, however. That was you.
I never imagined that

rivulets of hair could fall
so easily shoulder low,
or that irises could go

so deep and give the hue of
walnuts. I could not dream the
dream, in other words, amid

the progeny of warrior
gods, of one red jasmine woman,
my terra-cotta Seminole.

Manna

I do remember some things
times when I listened and heard
no one saying no, certain
miraculous provisions
of the much prayed for manna
and once a man, it was two
o'clock in the morning in
Pittsburg, Kansas, I finally
coming home from the loveliest
drunk of them all, a train chugged,
goddamn, struggled across a
prairie intersection and
a man from the caboose really waved, honestly, and said,
and said something like my name.

Death on Columbus Day

Sometimes you can hear the naked will
working, like the ocean becoming a shore
yesterday, and the day before,
the trees shrinking away,
even the mere transitional phase of seasons,
the tenacious skidding of a gone summer,
the cleaving to lusciousness,
and (you can see all this
from your window if you wash it
regularly, if you are afraid to go out)
even whole environments,
giants of varying kindness,
dissolve, and you, your pupils,
yes, blue as they may appear,
are, when you think about it,
acolytes to all destruction.

The Freak

In herds you slither about
the town: these are comfortable
moments for your mangled

gathering. How proudly you wear
your mange. It is the prime
mover of your awkward step.

Even the streetlights shy away
from the love you have for those
less recognizably human

than yourself. When alone, you
keep the corners of the world;
and, when at last relaxed there,

your pink, scarred paws explore
your broken parts. No one
to ask you now what beauty means

to you, just how much of it
you have to offer others.

The Last Letter from Old Kampoukos

I am feeling fine
at the present time.

I wish and hope both
of yours be the same.

I received your nice
and wonderful letter.

We was very happy
to hear from your people.

Well, my friend Aleck,
we feel the same way

about yours people –
because first the distance

is so far away, second
we can't eforted to make

trips back and ford, it
is not so easy for us. Etc. –

Well Aleck we live with
hops. We might see or meet

again on the future. No
doubt nowadays there is

really tough and rough
winter so cold probably

Zero. But you got to take it
just like the last winter.

The only thing you not
be able to go fishing.

But I think is excellent
weather for hunting HARE-Rapits.

You said yours son Leonidas
he get better position.

I suppose he get more money –
we are glad to hear that.

And we wish better lucky
to him. To have good life

and good success at his
future. Also we wish better

lucky to yours daughter
Cath at her future life.

About our friend Steve.
He is going to stay home.

He should take care of
himself. Etc. – Well Aleck

Mike he getting better.
He visit the Doctor five

times. His eye is all right
now. I believe he think

to take a trip to see
Neohorion once more.

The Birth place. But he
is not so sure yet. He not

decide. Well Aleck
you know and you realize

yourself we getting old
and weak – every year.

And every short time some
thing going out of commission.

We need Repairs!!!!!!
But is God's will or Nature.

The climate here is not
so bad little Rain.

The temperature is 60%
or 65% above – we don't

have cold – snow either Zero!!!
I hope the letter to find

both of yours on good
health. Offer my best

regards to your beloved
Wife Hazel. She is a nice

and wonderful Lady. Also
say Hello to Steve if you

see him. Etc. – Mike said
Hello to yours people.

God Blessed both of yours –
Good Lucky.

Very Truly – Yours.
Sincerely. Friendly –

Good Night,
George Kampoukos.

P.S.

Well Aleck taken easily
and both of yours take

care of yourself. Keep
warm shot W H I S K I

once an while – and don't
so much work round

the house. And have
little enjoyment according

to our age. Etc. –
Another month Spring

be around there. . . .

The Book of Lies

I'd like to have a word
with you. Could we be alone
for a minute? I have been lying
until now. Do you believe

I believe myself? Do you believe
yourself when you believe me? Lying
is natural. Forgive me. Could we be alone
forever? Forgive us all. The word

is my enemy. I have never been alone;
bribes, betrayals. I am lying
even now. Can you believe
that? I give you my word.

Miss Cho Composes in the Cafeteria

You are so small, I
am not even sure
that you are at all.

To you, I know I
am not here: you are
rapt in writing a

syllabic poem
about gigantic,
gaudy Christmas trees.

You will send it home
to China, and they
will worry about

you alone amid
such strange customs. You
count on your tiny

bamboo fingers; one,
two, three – up to five,
and, oh, you have one

syllable too much.
You shake your head in
dismay, look back up

to the tree to see
if, perhaps, there might
exist another

word that would describe
the horror of this
towering, tinselled

symbol. And . . . now
you've got it! You jot
it down, jump up, look

at me and giggle.

Sleeves

The shadow of a bleeding
defeated lion asleep
beneath a cedar tree, still

visibly afraid, confronts
me. Or, no, the way the eyes
are locked reflects shame.

He's not what he had thought.
This happens. I saw a brute
at a party. He was going

to lift a goddess of
beauty with each glad hand.
Prefatory entertainment:

the bully blushed and prepared
to flex his lauded arms, found
his sleeves completely empty.

The Mirror

She tells me
that I can
see right through
her, but I
look and can
see nothing:

so we go
ahead and
kiss. She is
fine glass, I
say, throwing
her to the
floor. . . .

The Tabernacle

Poor God was always there,
but He was something sinister,
and we worshiped the fear

we had of Him,
we had of the church on Tenth,
near the end

of the whole dark city.
The way the family
gathered murmuring on a Sunday,

surreptitious, solemn,
down to the midwest harlem
to give our worn

and rusty souls an airing –
grandmother swearing
at Ruthanna's hoop ear-rings,

and Uncle Barrington,
hesitant, knowing what would come,
stealing his Sunday swill of rum

invariably. Once there, it was not
as bad as we had thought;
it was not God at all, but

Pentecostal
joy. A man would wrestle
with his soul, and all

the other sinners cheered,
and soon we heard
the voices of another tongue –

garbled, and far too
inflated for us
to understand who

taught them how to sing such songs.

The Guests

Our house was strewn with
people whom no one claimed
to know, people who had

been there for thirty years
or more. One might show
himself at dinner, cobwebbed

and thinner than the dead.
No one would speak of it,
unless the guest became

unpleasant, and then it was
in gestures, because our
voices were saved for something

better. Our dry lips flecked
with foam, our hammering hearts
out-waited our guests, and

now, at last, we are alone.

Late Harvest

I look up and see
a white buffalo
emerging from the
enormous red gates
of a cattle truck
lumbering into
the mouth of the sun.
The prairie chickens
do not seem to fear
me; neither do the
girls in cellophane
fields, near me, hear me
changing the flat tire
on my black tractor.
I consider screaming
to them; then, night comes.

The Eye of Hurricane Renée

Today the clouds are
become vats of soda.
I keep poor company
with myself. There
is inflation
in the temporal sequence
of significant events,
I say to myself
out of ennui.

When I came in,
Don said they were
just going out, but
that I could stay
and read/listen
to the bad music.

I am sitting here
thinking that there
must still be some
value in thought.

What are you thinking?

Today I Am Falling

A sodium pentothal landscape,
a bud about to break open –
I want to be there, ambassador
to the visiting blossoms, first
to breathe their smothered, secret
odors. Today I am falling, falling,
falling in love, and desire
to leave this place forever.